The Classical Piano Sheet Music Series

INTERMEDIATE
BEETHOVEN
FAVORITES

ISBN 978-1-70517-226-1

HAL•LEONARD®

Visit Hal Leonard Online at
www.halleonard.com

World headquarters, contact:
Hal Leonard
7777 West Bluemound Road
Milwaukee, WI 53213
Email: info@halleonard.com

In Europe, contact:
Hal Leonard Europe Limited
1 Red Place
London, W1K 6PL
Email: info@halleonardeurope.com

In Australia, contact:
Hal Leonard Australia Pty. Ltd.
4 Lentara Court
Cheltenham, Victoria, 3192 Australia
Email: info@halleonard.com.au

Contents

All musical markings in brackets are editorial additions.

Bagatelle in A minor
("Für Elise")

Ludwig van Beethoven
WoO 59

*Traditionally played as D; E in the manuscript and first edition.
Fingerings are editorial suggestions.

*See footnote on p. 4.

*See footnote on p. 4.
**Some editions have:

*See footnote on p. 4.

**Alternately:

Bagatelle in B-flat Major

Ludwig van Beethoven
WoO 60

Ziemlich lebhaft

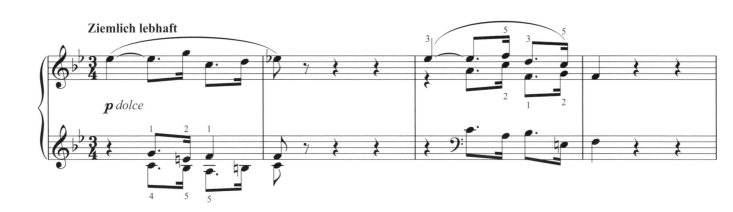

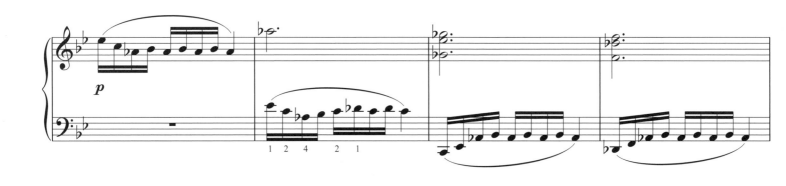

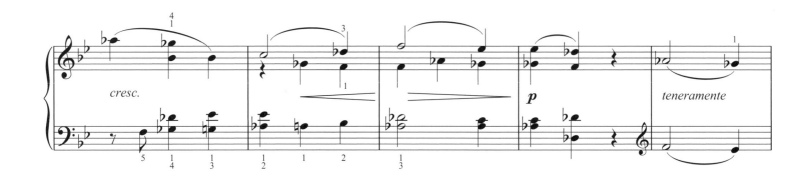

Bagatelle in C Major

Ludwig van Beethoven
Op. 33, No. 2

Bagatelle in A Major

Ludwig van Beethoven
Op. 33, No. 4

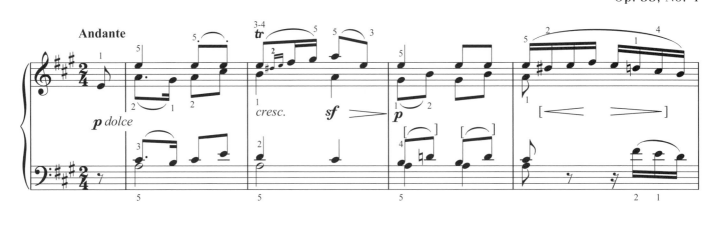

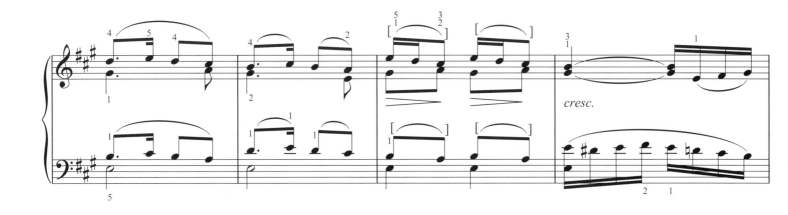

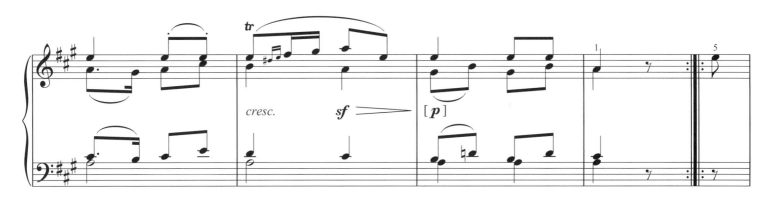

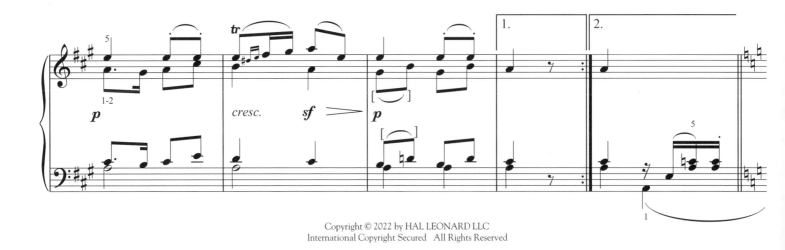

Bagatelle in D Major

Ludwig van Beethoven
Op. 33, No. 6

Allegretto quasi Andante
Con una certa espressione parlante

Bagatelle in A-flat Major

Ludwig van Beethoven
Op. 33, No. 7

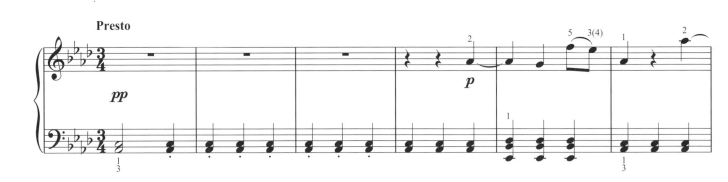

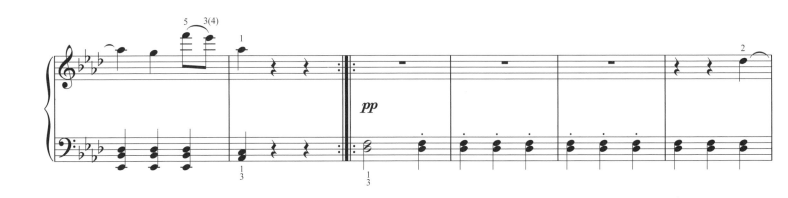

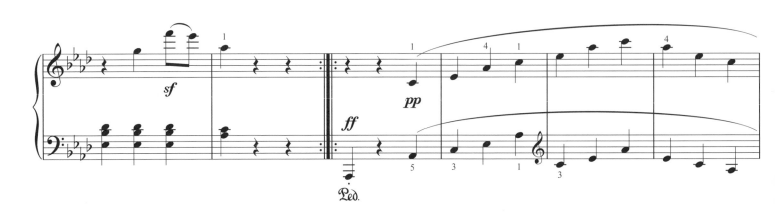

Bagatelle in G minor

Ludwig van Beethoven
Op. 119, No. 1

Allegretto

Bagatelle in A Major

Ludwig van Beethoven
Op. 119, No. 4

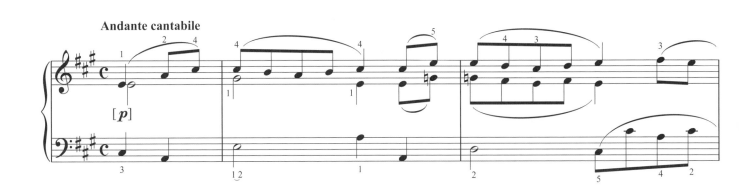

Bagatelle in C minor

Ludwig van Beethoven
Op. 119, No. 5

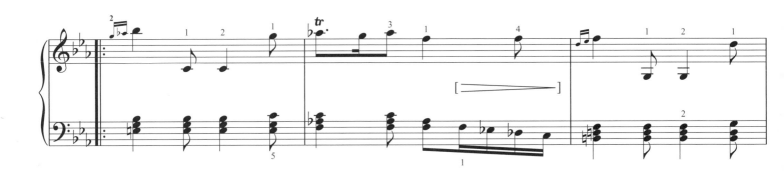

Bagatelle in C Major

Ludwig van Beethoven
Op. 119, No. 8

Bagatelle in A minor

Ludwig van Beethoven
Op. 119, No. 9

Vivace moderato

Bagatelle in A Major

Ludwig van Beethoven
Op. 119, No. 10

Bagatelle in B-flat Major

Ludwig van Beethoven
Op. 119, No. 11

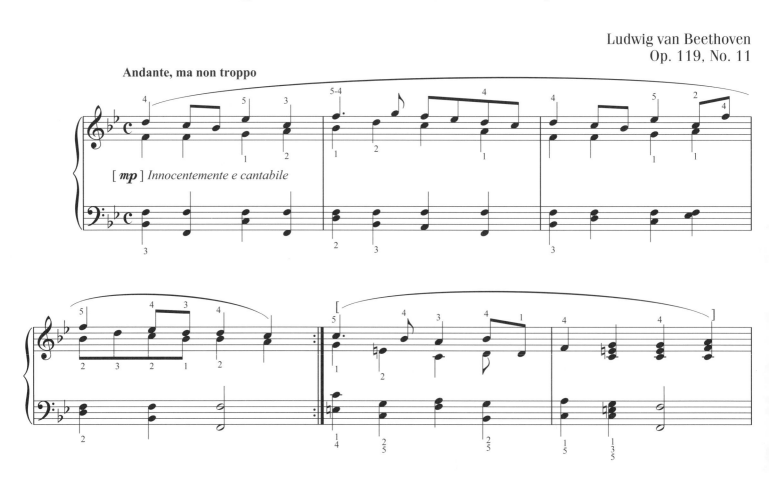

Bagatelle in G Major

Ludwig van Beethoven
Op. 126, No. 5

Ecossaise in G Major

Ludwig van Beethoven
WoO 23

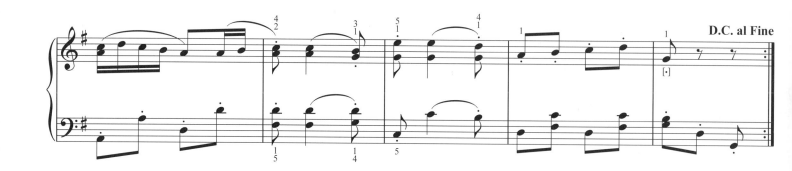

Ecossaise in E-flat Major

Ludwig van Beethoven
WoO 86

German Dance in G Major

Ludwig van Beethoven
WoO 8, No. 6

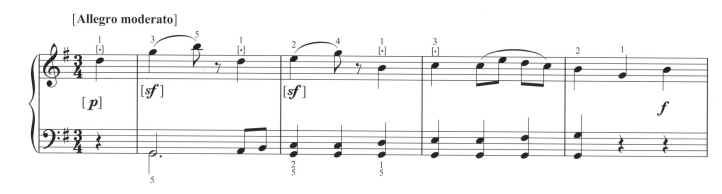

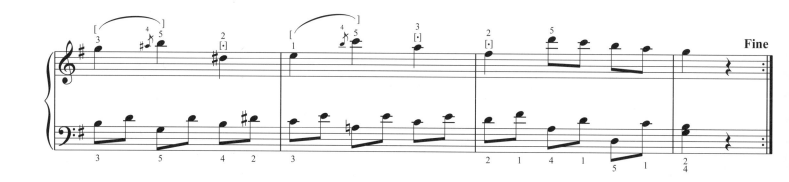

Trio

D.C. al Fine
senza repetizione

German Dance in C Major

Ludwig van Beethoven
WoO 8, No. 7

[Allegro moderato]

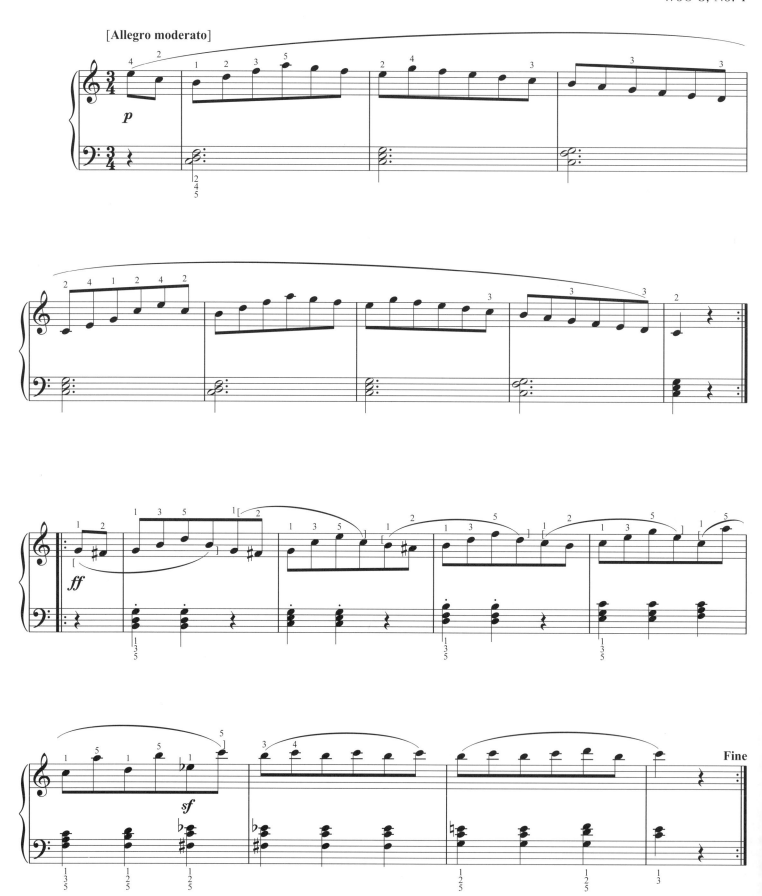

Trio

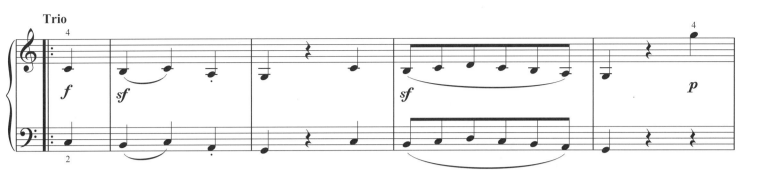

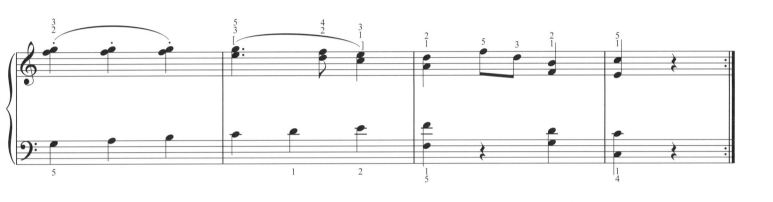

D.C. al Fine
senza repetizione

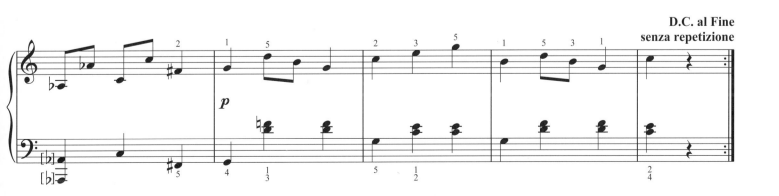

German Dance in G Major

Ludwig van Beethoven
WoO 8, No. 11

Trio

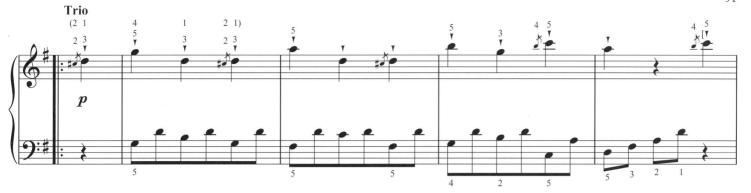

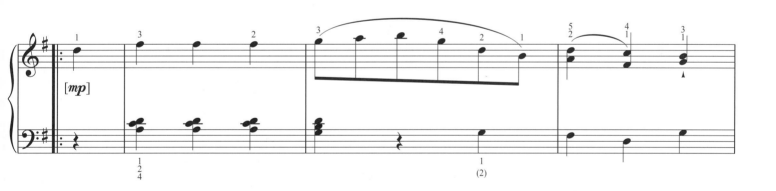

D.C. al Fine
senza repetizione

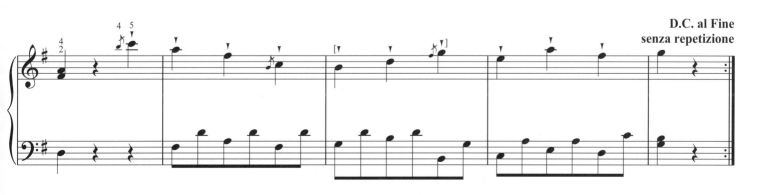

German Dance in B-flat Major

Ludwig van Beethoven
WoO 13, No. 2

[Allegro moderato]

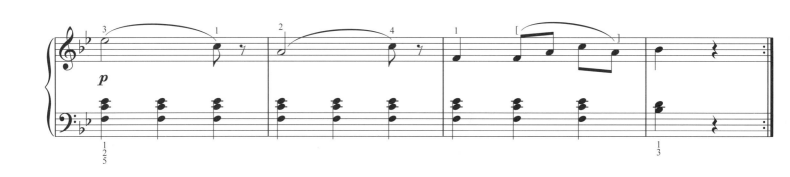

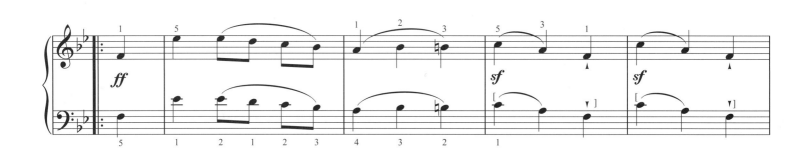

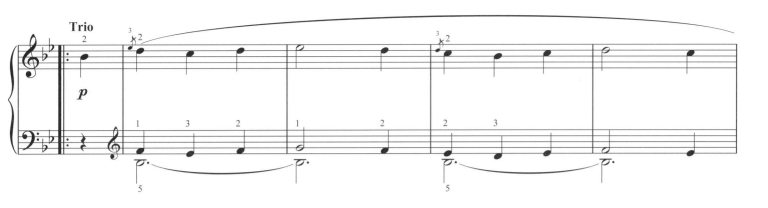

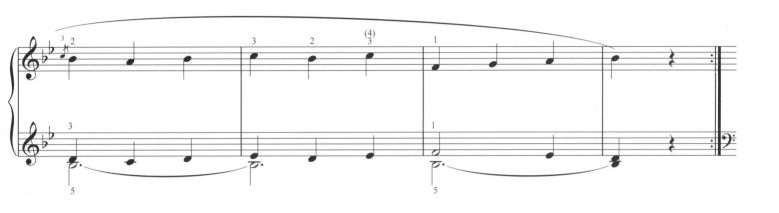

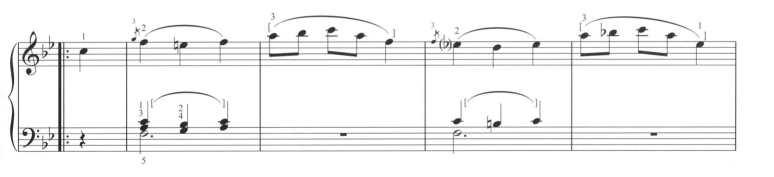

D.C. al Fine
senza repetizione

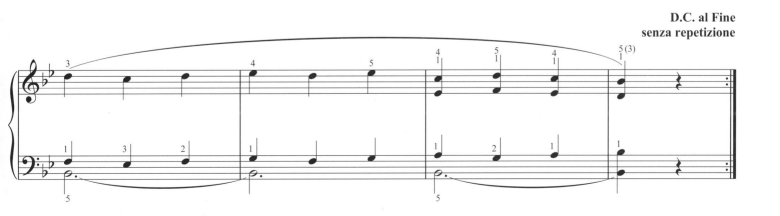

German Dance in C Major

Ludwig van Beethoven
WoO 8, No. 1

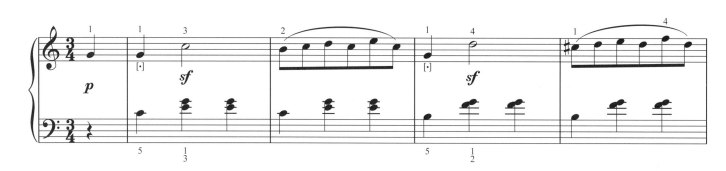

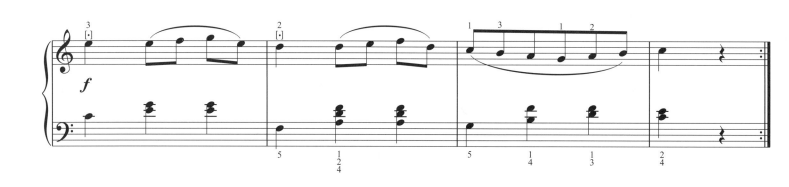

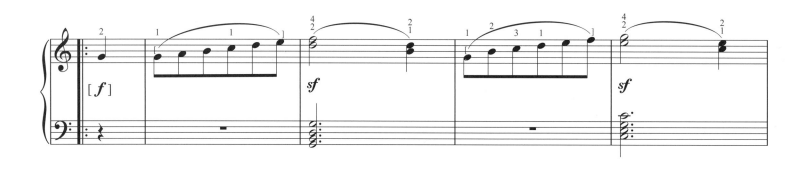

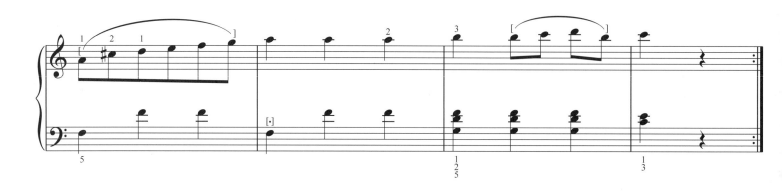

Landler in D Major

Ludwig van Beethoven
WoO 11, No. 4

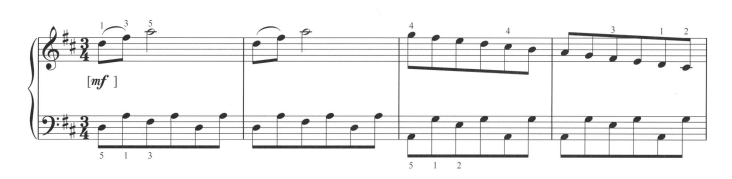

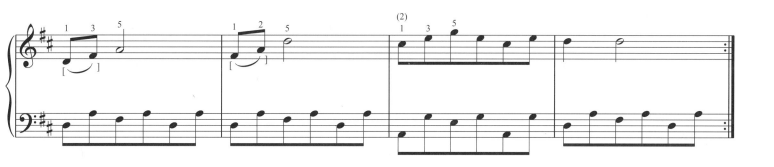

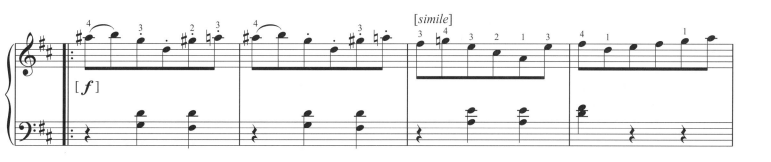

Landler in D Major

Ludwig van Beethoven
WoO 11, No. 2

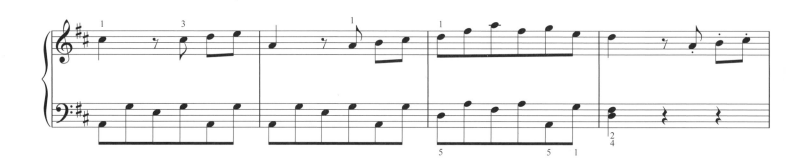

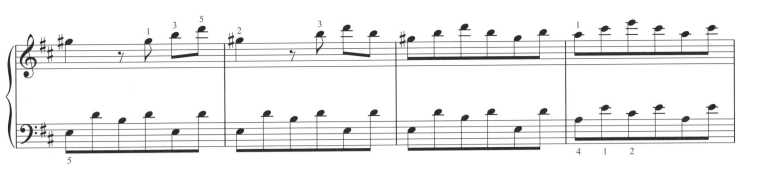

Landler in D Major

Ludwig van Beethoven
WoO 11, No. 7

Landler in D Major

Ludwig van Beethoven
WoO 15, No. 2

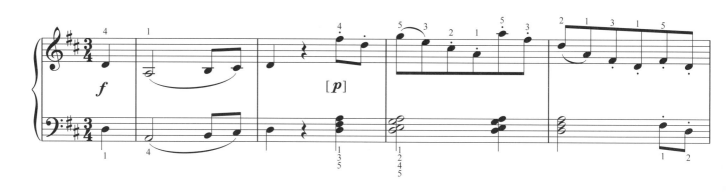

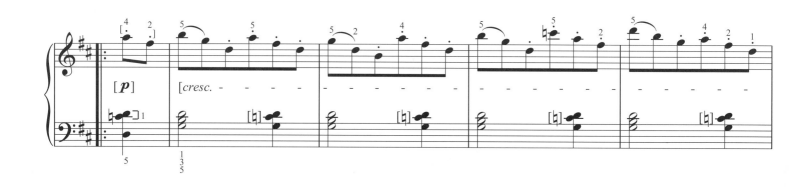

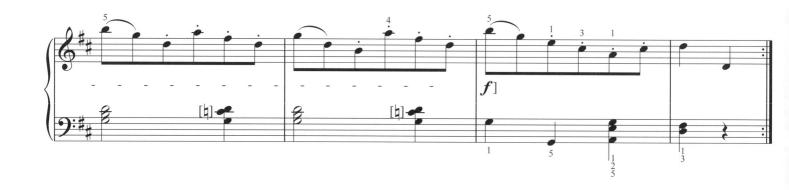

Landler in D minor

Ludwig van Beethoven
WoO 15, No. 4

Menuet in B-flat Major

Ludwig van Beethoven
WoO 7, No. 8

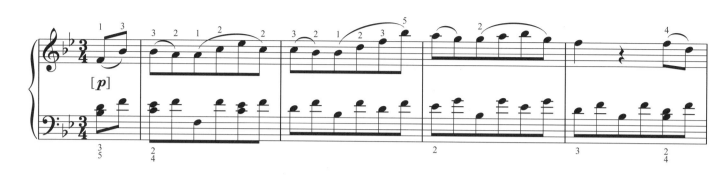

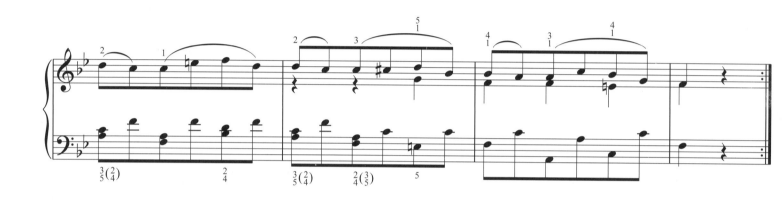

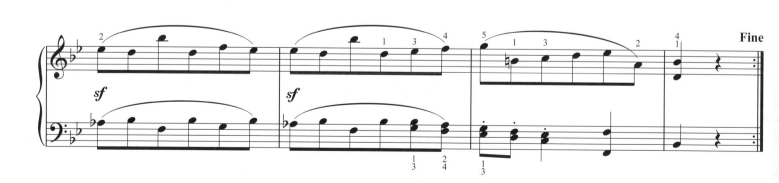

Sonata in G minor

I

Ludwig van Beethoven
Opus 49, No. 1

Andante [♩ = 69]

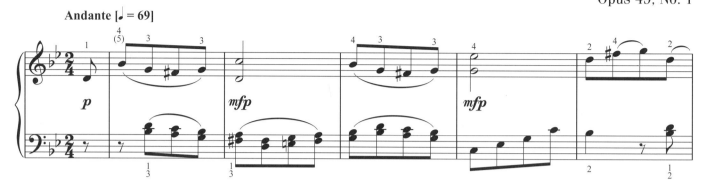

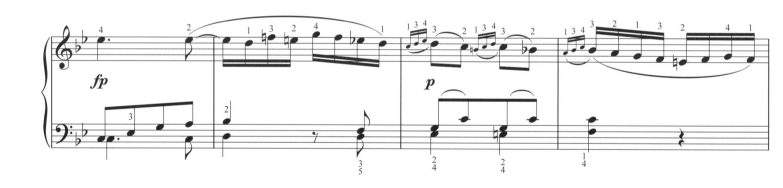

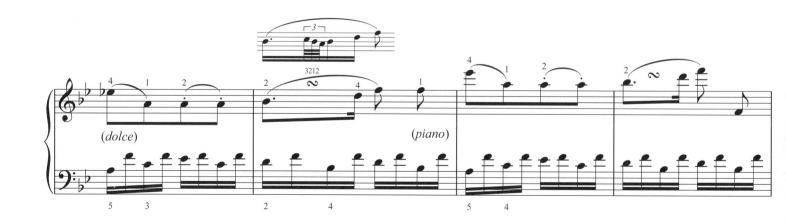

*without tail (ohne Nachschlag)

68

II

Rondo
Allegro [♩. = 92]

74

Sonata in G Major

I

Ludwig van Beethoven
Opus 49, No. 2

Allegro, ma non troppo [♩ = 76]

*There are no dynamic markings included in the first edition (Kunst und Industrie-Comptoir,
Vienna, 1805). All dynamic markings in this sonata are suggestions of the current editor.

*without tail (ohne Nachschlag)

II

Tempo di Menuetto [♩ = 100]

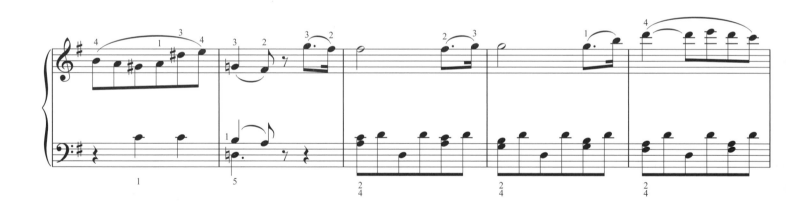

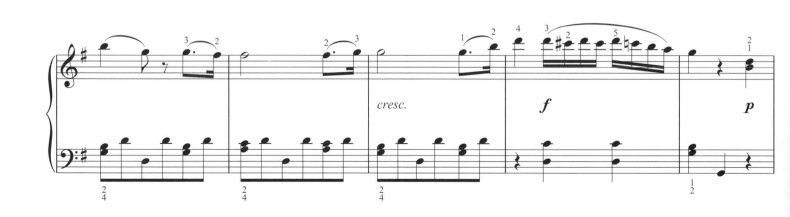

Rondo in C Major

Ludwig van Beethoven
Op. 51, No. 1